I0480292

TABLE OF CONTENTS

INTRODUCTION

Congratulations for downloading this eBook, and thank you for doing so. Many people wish that they could work from home. However, most people believe that the only way to generate a viable income that you can use to support yourself is to go to work every day. However, a few people believe that a goal such as working from home is attainable.

If you spend any amount of time browsing the internet, you have probably seen quite a few ads that promise that you can earn hundreds of thousands of dollars working from home. However, you are smart enough to know that those scams are too good to be true. And they are. But don't let those numerous scams stop you from reaching your goal.

How to

Make Money

from Home

How To Make Money From Your Computer
At Home For Beginners

The purpose of this eBook is to explain to you real and viable options that you have for working from home. They range from part-time and per-diem gigs to full-time options that can generate a livable salary. This eBook will begin by talking about the reasons people want to work from home, some of the benefits to working from home, as well as some of the drawbacks. It will then describe different approaches that you can take to working from home. You can freelance, and there are many different types of freelancing. You can start a business. You can find ways to generate passive income. You can also look for a job that allows you to work full-time but remotely.

Whatever reason you have for wanting to work from home, this eBook will help give you the information that you need in order to make that goal a reality. Best of luck to you as you pursue the lifestyle that you want by not being tied down to a nine-to-five.

CHAPTER ONE

Making Money from Home

If you are reading this eBook, you probably want to know different ways that you can make money from home. You have your own reasons for wanting to know. Maybe you are tired of your day job — working nine to five to make someone else rich, annoying colleagues, and an overbearing boss can get to the best of us. Maybe you want the freedom and flexibility to be able to do things like travel or even take a year-long sabbatical. Maybe you are preparing for a major lifestyle shift, such as the birth or adoption of a child. Maybe you just want to be at home more so that you can dedicate more of your time and yourself to your family. Maybe you are looking for ways to supplement your income from work so that you can get out of debt and save.

Whatever your reason, this book will help you understand the different options that are available to help you make money from home.

Working from home has many benefits. Usually, you get to set your own schedule. You don't have to wake up and catch the bus or train to your nine-to-five. If you're a night owl, you can work in the middle of the night. If you're an early bird, you can wake up at five or six in the morning and get through all of your work by noon. You don't have to spend time waiting on co-workers to get things done so that you can do your job; therefore, working from home independently can be much more efficient. You can get all of your work done in a much shorter amount of time. You can get tax breaks from having a home office. Unless you have an important video call, you don't have to get dressed in your usual business casual attire. This alone can save you hundreds of dollars every year in wardrobe expenses! You don't have to worry about a commute to and from work, saving you both time and money. You can work while you are traveling, provided you have an internet connection.

Working from home also has its drawbacks. You have to be disciplined enough to get out of bed and get your work done without anybody telling you to do so. You have to be motivated enough that you are able to get work done on deadlines without someone continually checking up on you. You don't have colleagues to socialize with, which can be a bigger drawback than many people realize. If you work as a contractor, you will have to set money aside every month for taxes because your employer won't be deducting them from your monthly salary. You will also have to pay a self-employment tax, which can be hefty, depending on your income.

Before you read any further, there is an important caveat. Working from home is still work. You won't be getting paid to wake up at noon and take surveys in your pajamas while eating ramen noodles or cereal. You have to be very disciplined and motivated, perhaps even more so than if you were working a traditional job. If you are looking for an easy way to make passive money without even trying, you might want to stop reading now. However, if you are prepared to roll up your sleeves and do the same amount of work that you are used to, just from home instead of an office, then keep reading. This book could be the key to changing your entire lifestyle.

If you have done a Google search of ways to work from home, you have probably come up with a number of scams that promise you can make fast money without even trying. Plenty of ads claim that you can make a thousand dollars a day. If you click on those links, you will find that you are no closer to being able to work from home, but your computer may be infected with all kinds of viruses. However, you don't need to be discouraged. There are many ways that you can work from home. You just need to know the right places to look. This book will show you those places, as well as give you some ideas about different paths that you could take.

Incomes from working at home can vary widely. If you find a job that is full time, you may or may not be able to pull the same salary as if you were working full time in an office. Be aware that a lot of companies hire people to work remotely as a way of saving money, both in office space and in salaries. Most jobs that you find will probably be freelance or contracting-based, meaning that they are not full time and your hours and income are not guaranteed. Those kinds of jobs enable you to put your skills to good use and are great as supplements to a steady source of income, such as that from your day job.

There are ways that you can start your own business online, provided you have some start-up capital. As many people have found out, starting your own business is not a foolproof way to a guaranteed income. You can do everything right and your business still either fail or not be as successful as you had hoped. However, your business can also thrive and bring in a sizable amount of income every month, freeing you up to have more of the lifestyle that you want.

CHAPTER TWO

Freelancing

Some people look at freelancing as something that desperate people do when they are unable to get a good job. It's something to do just for now, in the meantime, as opposed to a viable career path that can open up a lot of opportunities. While many freelancers are college students who need to earn some money to pay for food or a weekend trip, more than a few freelancers are adults with undergraduate and even graduate degrees who have found that it is a way to having a lifestyle of freedom from the daily grind.

There are many different ways to freelance. By definition, freelancing means that you offer your services to business and individuals, usually to multiple clients at a time.

The challenge is not in finding your own niche or skill that you can apply as a freelancer but in finding business and individuals that you can take on as clients. Successful full-time freelancers have a polished resume and market themselves online so as to attract new clients. They also have a history of clients who go back to them for additional services and who recommend them to other potential new clients. With these things in mind, getting a start as a freelancer can be a challenge. Many experts recommend that unless you have a work and/or educational history that clearly qualifies you (meaning that you are beginning with a superior resume and can easily establish a viable online presence), you should be realistic with yourself. Step back and take a reality check. Before you quit your day job, start out part-time. Try to get some clients. Get their reviews and use them to start up your website advertising yourself. Otherwise, you may quickly find yourself both out of your day job and out of any source of income.

This chapter will outline and describe different freelancing ideas and opportunities for different skill areas, as well as steps that you need to take in order to be able to work in those different niches.

Ghostwriting. Ghostwriting means that you are writing blogs, books, articles, or any other type of written media but not taking the credit for it.
Most famous people who have published books actually did not write the books. They don't have the time or the

skills necessary to put a book together. They actually use ghostwriters to write the books for them, then publish them under their own names. The ghostwriters who work for high-end clients are usually authors who have been published themselves and are looking for ways to continue putting their skills to good use. They can make as much as a dollar per word or even more. If you consider that most books nowadays must be 60,000-80,000 words, these ghostwriters are bringing in a sizable amount of income!

Other ghostwriters are hired by people who have a great idea for a story but, like many high-profile individuals who publish books, don't have the time or skills necessary to put a book together. They may have a full outline of a story or nonfiction book

Some ghostwriters are hired by companies to write eBooks or online content, such as blogs or advertising materials.

Possibly the lowest level of ghostwriting is for high school or college students who don't have the time or motivation to do their class assignments. Some unscrupulous individuals will place ads on sites such as Craigslist looking for someone to do their assignments for them. Stay away from clients such as these.
Odds are, you won't even get paid for your work.

One way to get started as a ghostwriter is to apply with

a ghostwriting company, which will find the clients for you. This can be a great way to build up a clientele, reputation, and resume without having to worry too much about the business side of things. You will be able to focus almost exclusively on the writing. The amount that ghostwriting companies pay will vary considerably, depending on factors such as the clientele and audience of the text to be ghostwritten. Another way is to advertise yourself on a freelancing website, such as www.freelancer.com, and apply for gigs. Every time that you are hired and complete a project, your clients can post reviews. This is a great way to build up your resume. Another way to get started as a ghostwriter is to scour sites such as Craigslist. Oftentimes companies will post ads looking for one-time ghostwriters to do a gig or project for them. This method can be great if you are looking for some extra side income but don't want to ghostwrite full time. However, you need to consider the fact that if you are not connected to a ghostwriting company, you need to have a very clear and notarized contract with the company that hired you to do ghostwriting. Otherwise, you have no guarantee that you will be paid for your work.

If you work as a ghostwriter, you get paid for your work, sometimes very handsomely.
However, you don't get any credit for it. If the work goes on to be published and receives substantial royalties, unless a contract stating the opposite was signed before you began work, you will not receive any of those royalties.

Those things said, ghostwriting is an excellent freelancing opportunity for people who are gifted as writers and want to put their talents to good use.

Editing. Editing is usually thought of as the process whereby someone proofreads texts for things such as grammar and spelling mistakes, as well as inconsistencies within the text. However, there are many different levels of editing. Developmental or concept-level editing refers to helping a writer develop the baseline of the story, such as characters, goals, and plot. For a nonfiction work, concept-level editing is the process of helping writers determine their goals of what they want to communicate and how they will do so. This level of editing is very broad and deals with the entire text from a bird's-eye view. It is the most intensive and has more in common with ghostwriting than with what is normally considered editing.

The next level of editing is substantive editing. While concept-level editing looks at the conceived-of text as a whole, substantive editing looks at the individual paragraphs. It is designed to help improve the structure of the paragraphs so that the entire text as a whole flows better. Substantive editing looks at things such as whether or not all of the sentences in a paragraph contribute to the overall theme that is being communicated, whether the paragraph has a clear theme, revision of sentences and information so that it best supports the theme, and removing what does not support it. The goal is to make sure that the information presented is communicated in the best and most organized way possible.

After substantive editing, the next level of editing is copy editing, which looks at the individual sentences of the text. At this level, significant changes are not made by the editor. Rather, he or she looks for redundancies, words that don't seem to fit or that could be replaced by a better word, grammar mistakes, and things like that.

After copy editing comes fact-checking editing. The purpose of this kind of editing is to make sure that all of the information in a text is correct. Nothing sinks a text faster than incorrect information! Oftentimes, fact-checking editors are skilled in a particular niche. For example, a Ph.D. student may want a fact-checking editor to review his or her dissertation. If the dissertation is on the role of a school in shaping a child's cultural identity, the Ph.D. student would probably not want to hire someone who studied marine biology! Fact-checking editors must be familiar with the topic and the sources available so that they are able to quickly and accurately determine whether or not the information presented in the text is true or not.

The final level of editing is proofreading. Proofreaders skim through a text looking for grammar and spelling mistakes, typos, formatting inconsistencies, and other detailed aspects of polishing a text.

Editors need to have a very strong grasp of the English language and be comfortable with understanding and communicating how to best communicate ideas in writing. If you have a degree in English and/or experience teaching it, such as in a junior high or high school classroom, editing may be a great freelance job for you.

Editors who work remotely can make a decent income, anywhere from a penny a word to ten dollars or more per page. However, you need to be aware that clients in need of editing services are usually on a deadline and need a quick turnaround. You need to be able to commit to doing the job quickly, efficiently, and accurately.

Like with ghostwriting, there are different ways that you can get started working as an editor. You can apply with a company that provides professional editing services, such as a copywriting company. Make sure that the company is one that is looking for people to work remotely; some editing companies are looking to hire people to work on-site. You can go through a freelancing website, such as www.freelancer.com. Through your account, you can advertise yourself and apply for different freelancing jobs as an editor. You could also look at websites such as Craigslist to find potential clients who are in need of editing services.

As with ghostwriting, editing is a niche field. Before you decide that editing is for you, you need to make sure that you are qualified for the job. Spend some time building up your resume, portfolio, and online presence so that you are better able to attract clients. Don't go into the field blindly, figuring that it will be an easy way to make money. If you are unqualified, any clients that you find will quickly find out. Your ratings will sink faster than the Titanic.

Photography. Maybe writing isn't for you. That's OK! There are plenty of non-writing freelancing niches that you can explore. If you are passionate about photography and already have a portfolio of high-quality, professional-level images, you may be able to make a small income from freelance photography. I say a small income because freelance photography really doesn't pay well. However, if it is something that you enjoy, you might as well make some money off of it!

There are quite a few jobs for photographers that are not freelance. For example, police and investigators need photographers for crime scenes. If you are looking to be a full-time freelance photographer, then you may want to begin on the side while working a full-time job that involves using your skills in photography.

There are many different reasons why clients might

need a photographer. Maybe a publishing company or a self-publishing author needs cover art for a book. Maybe a bride and groom need a photographer to capture their wedding. Maybe parents want a high-quality photo of their infant's baptism. Maybe an aspiring model needs headshots. The reasons are endless.

Many freelance photographers do photo shoots at the site of the client's choosing. Much of their advertising either are passed down through word of mouth from satisfied clients or from pictures being shared through social media sites, such as Facebook.

In order to successfully work as a freelance photographer, you need to be realistic about your goals. Are you trying to provide a full income through photography? If so, you may be unpleasantly surprised to find that freelance photography does not tend to pay very well unless you find yourself contracted by a high-profile publication, such as *National Geographic.*
Freelance photography can be a fun way to get out of your comfort zone and make some extra side cash.

There are some ways to get started as a freelance photographer. You could find a company that specializes in freelance photography and contract to work with it per diem. You could scour freelancing sites, such as www.freelancer.com, to look for gigs as a photographer. You could also go to networking sites, such as Craigslist, to look for gigs.

There are some things that you need in order to build up a clientele. One is a website that is consistently updated with new photographs. If any potential client is interested in hiring you, your website is probably the first place that he or she will check. It's the place to really broadcast both your skills as a photographer and the breadth of subjects that you have photographed. Another thing that you will need is a high-quality camera, for obvious reasons. Perhaps the most important thing that you will need is a network of people and the ability to work that network in order to bring in potential clients. Your first clients and many thereafter may come from your social circles.

If you want to move from freelance photography as a side gig to a full-time career, you will want to use your network to have shows of your photography. See if your friends can send samples of your work to potential buyers. A local coffee shop or diner can be a great place to have the first show. As your clientele grows (hopefully along with your budget), you can move to more upscale venues, such as local libraries and museums.

If you want to do full-time freelance photography, you will also want to send samples of your work to major publications that may be in need of photographers. Make sure that any work that you send them comes with your contact information and a link to your website. You will also want to enter photography contests to help build up your resume.

Transcription. Much of the aforementioned work involves a degree of creativity and/or passion for the work. Transcription, on the other hand, is perfect for a type A personality or anyone who doesn't want to have to invest too much creative energy in work. While some people find repetitive work such as transcription to be repetitive and dull, some people find it to be Zen and soothing. If you are one of the latter, transcription may be a great work-from-home option for you.

Transcription is the process of taking either a sound recording or a handwritten text and turning it into a typed file. To be a successful transcriptionist, the most important skill you need is the ability to type quickly and accurately, preferably at least sixty words per minute.
Ninety words per minute is ideal.

Many companies and organizations want their sound files to be transcribed for several reasons. One reason is that outdated technology means that in a few years, the technology in which those sound files are stored may be completely obsolete and the information inaccessible. Another reason is that they want to best preserve the information for posterity; this is especially the case for oral history projects. Another reason is that they want to be able to make notes on a written document; taking notes on a sound file is cumbersome, if not impossible.

Some types of transcription require technical jargon. Oftentimes, Ph. D. students need someone to transcribe interviews from field research that they have done. Doctors and other healthcare practitioners need someone to transcribe many of their voice-recorded reports, interviews with patients, and other sound files. This niche is called medical transcription. While you don't necessarily need to be a healthcare professional or a Ph. D. in order to transcribe more technical files, you do need to be willing to learn some of the terminologies that you will encounter. Transcriptionists need a reliable internet connection so that they can look up words that they are not familiar with.

Transcription work can be very repetitive. Transcriptionists frequently need to rewind the sound file because they need to either make sure that they heard the words correctly or because the words are difficult to decipher. Some sound files can be of particularly poor quality, or the speakers may have heavy accents. Sometimes there may be multiple speakers, and discerning between the different voices can be a challenge. Transcriptionists need to constantly go back and check their work to ensure that it is of the highest quality.

Transcriptionists must be very detail-oriented. Some companies will insist that the transcript must match up exactly word-for-word; any aberration could mean that they will never use you for any other work. To work as a transcriptionist, you must be able to ensure that your work is entirely free from error.

Another challenge associated with transcription work is that spoken language can differ substantially from written language. For example, we don't necessarily speak in complete sentences or use proper grammar. However, a transcriptionist must be able to convert the spoken word into the written word. For this reason, as well as the aforementioned ones, if you want to work as a transcriptionist, you need to be very clear with your client exactly what is expected from the transcript. Does the client want the transcript to be exactly verbatim, including uhs, ums, and filler words such as like, kind of, or you know? Does the client want a modified verbatim, excluding these prompts but still a literal representation of what was spoken? Does the client want the text to be modified so as to represent written communication instead of spoken communication? These are important questions to be answered.

If you want to work from home as a freelance transcriptionist, there are several ways to get started. One way is to find a company that specializes in transcription work and hires outside contractors. These companies will generally require that you submit the results of an online typing test to prove that you can accurately type at a certain rate. They will probably also require you to transcribe a sample text, for which you will not get paid. The sample text will probably contain some kind of difficulties, such as a heavy accent or poor audio quality. If you pass the approval process, you will be able to take as much or as little transcription work as you want, provided work is available by the company. If you are available to transcribe three hours of audio one week, let the company know. If you are available to transcribe ten hours of audio one week, let the company know. If you are reliable and available, you should find a steady stream of work. However, there is one caveat to keep in mind. Many transcription companies hire contractors to work for supplemental income; they do not intend for contractors to be looking for full-time or primary income. If you want to work full time as a transcriptionist, consider contracting with two companies simultaneously.

Another way to get started working as a transcriptionist is to go through freelance websites, such as www.freelancer.com. You can also go through sites such as Craigslist to find transcription gigs. Oftentimes, companies will post ads on Craigslist because they want to hire an individual rather than pay more money to go through a transcription company. You can also advertise yourself at a local university; this method will probably be effective only if it has Ph. D. students.

Transcription work usually pays between fifty cents and one dollar per minute of audio, depending on factors such as the client, the quality of the sound recording, and your experience at transcription. As a general rule, the more that you are paid for a transcription job, the higher the degree of perfection that the client will require of you.

These are just a few examples of jobs that you can work as a freelancer. Based on your own unique skills and qualifications, the possibilities of jobs that you can work could be much bigger. For example, if you are a nurse, you could work as a traveling nurse. Traveling nurses go to different hospitals and nursing homes around the country for a particular assignment of a limited time, usually a few weeks to months. They tend to get paid much more than regularly staffed nurses, but also get to travel and see the world.

Maybe you have an entirely unique skill that you could market to earn money as a freelancer. For example, you might be a fantastic cake baker and decorator but aren't interested in working for a bakery. You could network through your social circles to find opportunities to create cakes for things such as birthday parties, anniversaries, and weddings. While you may not be able to generate a full salary, you can probably earn some cash on the side. The possibilities truly are endless.

CHAPTER THREE

Start Your Own Business

Starting your own business is one of the best ways to be able to work from home. It can be both a risky venture, as there is no guarantee that your business will succeed, but also a rewarding one. When you build your business from the ground up and see it take off, you will feel a surge of pride that is hard to describe. Nowadays, there are many different ways to start your own business. This chapter will describe a few.

Sell products for an established company. There is a myriad of companies that rely on independent contractors to sell their goods. These contractors network with their own social circles to host parties, online forums, and find other marketing opportunities to sell their products. Companies that operate in this way include Rodan + Fields,

Avon, Mary Kay, Juice Plus, and Premier Jewelry. When you contract with these companies, you essentially begin your own business. You work to sell the products and receive a royalty or commission based on how much you sell.

Usually, you will have to make an up front monetary investment, such as purchasing a certain amount of the product that you will be selling, the rights to sell under that company's name, and introductory marketing materials. Some people find this as a deterrent to contracting with the company. Some, though, find it a necessary cost in order to be able to generate their own income on their own hours and work towards obtaining the lifestyle that they want.

Sell through an affiliate website. Websites such as eBay and Amazon are full of people who have established businesses by selling their products through a store. The easiest way to build a business through an affiliate website is to purchase items in bulk and sell them. For example, you may find that a high-end hair straightener costs $150 on its own, but you can buy it in bulk for $80. You would order a wholesale amount of the hair straighteners, store them at your own location (probably your house), and list them on the affiliate website. Every time an order is made, you would prepare the products to be shipped.

There are other, more creative ways to develop a

business on sites such as eBay. Maybe you are a fan of flea markets, pawn shops, and curiosity shops, and have an eye for rare, unique, and/or valuable objects. You could routinely scour your favorite stores and markets for objects that catch your eye as being potentially valuable to collectors but that are being sold for well below what they are probably worth. After you procure them, you could put them on your eBay store.

If you are craftsy and enjoy things such as sewing, you could create a shop through a website such as Etsy. You will need to have a particular specialty, such as diaper bags or unique purses, that will cause your shop to stand out. People can place orders that you will then fulfill.

CHAPTER FOUR

Generate Passive Income

Passive income is money that you don't necessarily work for on a regular basis. Rather, you complete a project, such as self-publishing a book, and then get paid in royalties. There are several different ways that you can generate passive income over the internet; passive income can be a great way to supplement the work that you are already doing.

Write a book. If you have a viable platform, such as you have a blog with over a thousand followers or you are a practitioner with hundreds of clients, you could generate sizable passive income from writing a book.

Income from a book can come in several different ways. If you choose to self-publish through a venue such as Amazon's CreateSpace, you will receive royalties based on how many copies are sold. If you have a high-profile name, you could contract with a traditional, mainstream publisher to write a book. The publisher may opt to either pay you an advance up front or write a percentage of royalties into your contract. If you don't have a high-profile name, you can still contract with a mainstream publisher. You will just have a much harder time. You will first need to write the book, then find a literary agent to represent you. The agent will advise you on editing changes that you need to make to the book, then try to sell your book to a mainstream publisher. The publisher may offer you an advance on royalties, meaning that you get a check when an offer to publish your book is made. After the book is published, you will receive a percentage of sales as royalties.

Publish your materials. There are many websites available through which specialists in particular fields can publish materials that they have produced. For examples, the website www.teacherspayteachers.com is a forum where teachers can sell curriculum that they have designed and created to other teachers. The prices are usually substantially cheaper than buying through an educational company, and most of the proceeds go directly to the teacher who created it. If you work in a particular field and have produced materials for it, see if there is a website through which you can sell your work.

Create a YouTube video. Are you a singer or songwriter

trying to showcase your work on YouTube? Do you have some funny videos of your pet that put you and your friends in stitches every time you see them? Then you may be able to generate some passive income from YouTube. YouTube has a program called AdSense, which enables you to allow ads to appear on your video. In return, you get paid a nickel per view. You can allow up to three ads on your video; however, too many ads can quickly detract from the quality of the video and prevent people from watching it.

Use your photographs as stock photos. People are always looking for high-quality photographs that they can use in professional-level work. Companies need photographs to use on their web pages. Publishers need photographs to use as cover art. One place where they know that they can get photographs of the highest quality is from sites such as www.shutterstock.com and www.istockphoto.com.

If you are a gifted photographer and have quite a few photographs that are just sitting in your portfolio, you could generate some revenue by putting them on those websites. If someone wants to use your photo, that person must pay a fee to obtain the rights to it. You then receive a royalty or commission off of that fee. The more photographs you have and the more people who use them, the more money that you will earn without having to go to work for it every day.

Build an app. Apps have become such an integral part of our daily lives that we barely even notice whether or not we are using them. If you have a knack for computer programming and a few great ideas for apps that could really benefit people, then building an app (or two, or a dozen) could be another great way to build up some passive income. You could either make an app that people initially pay for, one that people pay for every year, or one that is free but can be upgraded for a fee. You could also add services to your app that people can pay for.

These are just a few examples of how you can build your own online business. What you can do is limited only by your time, skills, and imagination.

CHAPTER FIVE

Find a Home-Based Full-Time Job

Another option that you have in being able to work from home is to find a job that is designed to be remote. Companies often look for remote workers as a way of reducing their overhead expenses; if you are working from home on your own computer and in your own home office, then the company doesn't have to provide for expenses such as a computer, internet connection, desk, or office space. The scenario is a win-win for both you and the company.

If you are interested in finding a full-time job that will

enable you to work from home, you would need to begin your search as you would any other job search. Go to sites such as www.monster.com and www.indeed.com, where employers post job vacancies. Search specifically for jobs that allow you to work remotely. Make sure that your resume is updated and polished and that you have good references before submitting it to any potential employers.

You can also go to websites such as Craigslist, where employers routinely post ads looking for workers. You can narrow your search specifically to look for jobs that are remote. Because Craigslist is local, meaning that you only search one city or metropolitan area at a time, you may want to search through several metropolitan areas. Even if you live in the heart of Texas, you can search for remote jobs that are based out of New York, Boston, Houston, Chicago, and Los Angeles, just to name a few cities. After all, working remotely means that you won't have to move in order to take the job.

Some remote jobs will still require you to maintain nine-to-five hours, for the purpose of things such as answering emails, collaborating with co-workers, and attending meetings via video calls. Be sure that you are clear if this is what is expected from the job for which you are applying.

Maybe it won't be a deterrent to you because you are less concerned about keeping certain hours and more concerned about being able to stay home with your children instead of commute. Maybe it will actually be helpful to you because you know that you may not be motivated and disciplined enough to maintain a full work schedule unless you have to be present for certain hours. However, if your reason for wanting to work online is specifically so that you can set your own schedule, then you should probably not pursue an option that requires you to be present online from nine to five.

An in-between option would be a company that is looking for workers who can work remotely some of the time and come into the office some of the time. This is a great way to get the best of both worlds. You would still have the benefit of being able to socialize and interact with colleagues, have a face-to-face relationship with your boss (which would enable you to better understand what he or she wants and expects from you), and collaborate in person on projects. On days that you don't go into the office, you have the benefits of not having to commute, being able to set your own schedule, and not having to wear business attire.

Maybe your current day job is one that you could work remotely, at least some of the time. If you think that working remotely might be a good option for your current job, maybe you could have a conversation with your boss in which you discuss that possibility. Be sure to play up the ways that you working remotely would benefit the company, such as freeing up your computer, desk, and office space for another worker. If you are preparing to move or do extensive traveling and are well-appreciated at work, your boss may actually offer to let you work remotely so that you won't have to be replaced!

CHAPTER SIX

Tips and Warnings

Hopefully, by now, you are brainstorming different ways that you can generate income working from home and are becoming more clear about what exactly you want from working from home. Maybe you just want some side gigs so as to generate some extra income. Maybe you want to be able to completely quit your day job so that you can pursue a totally different lifestyle. Before you begin working from home, there are some things that you should be aware of. This chapter will advise you on different things that you may not have been aware of before beginning to work from home.

Taxes. Mark Twain famously said that nothing in life is certain except for death and taxes. Even death is taxed! Any form of income is always taxed, so you need to be prepared for the fact that money that you earn from home will have to be reported to the IRS.

If you work as a contractor, the general rule is that you will not have to pay taxes on your income if the total for the year is less than $600. Hopefully, your goals are loftier than making $50 a month. There are specific tax laws related to working as an independent contractor, and you will probably have to fill out a different tax form. To the IRS, you will probably be considered a small business owner and be taxed as such.

If you are a freelancer, you will probably have to pay a self-employment tax. In traditional employment, your employer will have to pay, out of the business's income, a certain percentage of what you earn every pay period as a tax. Since freelancers have no employer, that payroll tax comes directly from them. You will need to keep very careful records of how much money you earn so that you can accurately report your earnings to the IRS and pay the appropriate amount of taxes. Failure to do so can result in you being audited, a rather painful and sometimes expensive process.

There are also specific deductions that you are able to take if you work from home. These include the cost of operating a home office; portions of your internet, phone, and utility bills; and any expenses that you may incur, such as having to purchase a new computer or phone. Know what deductions might be available to you and keep detailed records of expenses that can be deducted. If you take those deductions, the IRS will want to see receipts or other proof that you did incur those expenses during the tax year for the purposes of working from home. Being able to take advantage of these deductions can save you hundreds or even thousands of dollars come tax time.

Health insurance. Traditionally, health insurance is provided by employers. Health insurance companies are much more eager to ensure people who work full time because, as a general rule, they are healthy enough to be able to work full time. They are perceived to be less likely to have chronic diseases (otherwise, they would presumably have to miss a lot of work), presumably have healthier lifestyles than people who do not work, and are less susceptible to diseases. Employees who attain their health insurance through work may not even have to have a medical exam to guarantee their insurability.

Under Obamacare, an employer is required to cover the cost of health insurance, with some exceptions. The cost of insurance for full-time workers tends to be lower, for the aforementioned reasons. If you are not a full-time employee of a company, you will probably have to pay a lot of money for health insurance. Before you quit your full-time job and lose your health insurance, take a look at some health insurance quotes. You may find that your insurance will cost you upwards of $500, possibly even $1000 a month! Because of Obamacare, government subsidies are available to help you cover the cost of health insurance. Make sure you look into how much of a subsidy you would be able to receive based on what you project to earn working from home.

Make a schedule and stick to it. One of your reasons for working from home was probably the flexibility in your schedule that it would provide. While you may be enthusiastic for the first few days or weeks, you may soon find that your newfound freedom is a bit intoxicating. In fact, based on your personality, you may have trouble pulling yourself out of bed and getting any work done at all.

You need to set a schedule and stick to it. One benefit of working from home is that you can set your schedule according to what works best for you. You may decide to work every day from six in the morning until twelve noon, then spend the rest of the day catching up on your personal life. Great! Make sure that you do not neglect to give those six work hours your full and focused attention. You may decide to work every day from eight until eleven in the morning, and then from seven until eleven at night. Wonderful. Don't you love that you can set such an eccentric schedule and still get all your work done? Maybe your schedule will vary on different days of the week, based on when you need to pick your kids up or be at other commitments. Whatever works best for you, make a schedule and stick to it.

On that note, you also need to make sure that you are focused during work hours. Without having to worry about a boss looking over your shoulder, it can be easy to let ADD take over and instead of getting work done, spend your time surfing the web or watching videos of cats. Even though you are on your computer during your set work hours, your productivity is now zero. If your income is tied to your productivity, as most work-from-home jobs are, your income will also be zero. Do whatever you need to do in order to focus yourself to get your work done. Drink a cup of coffee or tea. Take a break when you feel that your productivity is slumping or you are getting tired. Stand up and walk around. Then get back to work.

If you cannot discipline yourself to work a certain number of hours every day or week, then working from home could be a dream-come-true-come-nightmare. You may find that you are not only out of your previous job, but that the lifestyle you had hoped working from home would bring is non-existent because you aren't able to actually bring in any money.

Stay motivated. Did you know that the least successful motivator to get people to work is money? That means that people who work so that they can earn a paycheck are usually miserable and don't like their jobs. The best motivator to work is having a job that is meaningful and fulfilling while allowing you to meet your own personal goals. Other motivators include having a boss that you like and want to please, the satisfaction of getting a job done, and having a meaningful professional relationship with co-workers.

That said, there are many, many benefits to being able to work from home, which have already been discussed. However, people don't tend to find work such as transcription or online data entry to be particularly meaningful. Rather, it is a simply a way to bring home money without having to go into the office. If you want to be successful at working from home in the long term, you need to find a way to motivate yourself. Maybe you can motivate yourself by posting a picture of a scene from your dream vacation above your desk. Maybe you can motivate yourself by keeping close tabs on how good a job you are doing at getting your credit card debt paid off. If you are working from home so that you can spend more time with your family, constantly remind yourself of how valuable your time with them is and that working from home allows you to be with them.

Get out of the house. One drawback of working from home is that you don't have as many reasons to leave the house. At first, this may sound fantastic, especially if you are a homebody. After all, who wants to have to go to work every day when you can just stay home and still work? However, after a few weeks or months, you may find yourself going a bit stir crazy from being cooped up inside all day. You may also find that you miss having co-workers to socialize with. You may soon find that you are actually becoming lonely. If you are finding these things to be true, then you need to find reasons to get out of the house and socialize.

One particular challenge in getting out of the house and socializing when you work from home is that people have such busy lives. During the day, most people that you would normally socialize with — your co-workers — are at work. Your friends are probably either busy at work, taking care of their kids, or being involved in community projects. In the evenings, when you have already been home all day and are looking for a reason to go out, a lot of people have been at work all day and want to stay at home.

You need to find a way to socialize that is compatible with your new lifestyle. Try to schedule a lunch date with a friend or significant other at least once a week. Invite people over for supper. Accept invitations to join people when they ask you to go out with them for an evening or the weekend. Sign up to work with a temp agency so that when work is slow, you can work for anywhere from a few hours to a few weeks somewhere outside of your house. Whatever you do, get out of the house and socialize. Do not let your dream of working from home turn into loneliness and depression.

Set an agenda for the day. As with any job, if you work from home there will be certain tasks that need to be completed each day. In a traditional workplace, many companies have periodic meetings in which employees are briefed on current needs and what is expected of them. You need to do the same thing for yourself. Brief yourself every morning on exactly what needs to get done that day. You may find that making a checklist every morning is a beneficial way of keeping track of what needs to get done. If you get through every item on your checklist before your scheduled time to "clock out," then you get to leave work early. That incentive should motivate you to get as much work done as possible!!

Maybe the client or online employer for which you are working doesn't have a set task that you need to complete today. In that case, it is up to you to motivate yourself to decide what needs to be done. Do you have a deadline that is coming up, even if it is days or weeks away? Ask yourself what you can do today to meet that deadline. Are you working on a large transcription project but don't need to turn anything in today or tomorrow? Maybe you are a freelance photographer trying to generate passive income from stock photos. Get out and take pictures. Give yourself a quota of how many pictures you should take each day. Figure out how much you need to get done in order to earn as much money today as you need.

Remember that when you don't have someone looking over your shoulder or keeping constant tabs on how much work you are getting done, you will have to motivate yourself. It can be tempting to not get any work done today, but once you start making a habit of not getting an adequate amount of work done every day, you will have a hard time getting back on course.

Get dressed. You may have decided to work from home so that you don't have to put on a business outfit every day. Maybe you were hoping that you could work in your pajamas whenever you wanted. That mindset needs to change. The clothes do make the person, not only because of how they affect how others perceive you but also how you perceive yourself. Think about this: You wear pajamas for sleeping. They are great for binge watching on Netflix while eating cookie dough ice cream and being all-around lazy. However, now you are at work. You cannot afford to waste any time by being lazy. Staying in your pajamas can actually cause you to waste time without you even realizing it.

Maybe you had pajama days at a traditional job because there were days when you were able to stay at home and work remotely. However, there is a huge difference between being able to work from home for a day here and there and working from home every single day for years.

So get dressed. You don't have to put on business attire. Blue jeans and a t-shirt will suffice. You don't have to fix your hair to look perfect, but you do need to brush it. The shift in productivity from wearing your pajamas to wearing actual clothes is tremendous. The simple act of putting clothes on can motivate you and get you into the mindset of needing to get work done. Also, if you need to take a break by getting out of the house, you are already dressed to do so.

CONCLUSION

As you can hopefully see by now, even though scams abound about how you can work from home, there are plenty of legitimate ways to work from home and generate a steady, legitimate income. After reading this eBook, you should be familiar with different things that you can do in order to begin working from home. After getting a realistic idea of what a home-based job would be like, you need to step back and reflect on what exactly you hope to gain from working from home. Side income to pay off debts or fund a dream vacation? Extra time to spend with your family and loved ones? A lifestyle that allows you to travel and see the world while still earning money?

Before you quit your day job, you need to sure that you will be able to generate adequate income by working from home. Don't go in blindly, believing the scams that say that you can earn a thousand dollars a day. If you want to work from home, you will have to work. You will also have to be disciplined and motivated enough to get all of your work done without having to constantly report to a boss or other superior.

While there are numerous benefits to working from home, make sure that you understand and are prepared for the challenges. For most people who are prepared, the benefits far outweigh the challenges and working from home is a choice that they will never regret. Best of luck to you on your new journey, and may all of your goals in working from home be fulfilled!

DESCRIPTION

Most people dream of being able to quit their jobs and work for themselves. They want to be able to work from home, set their own schedules, and live by their own rules. They want to get away from the daily grind and having to please "the man" and instead pursue their own personal goals, such as spending more time with family or being able to take a year-long sabbatical. If you are reading this, you are probably one of those people. Your reasons for wanting to quit your day job are your own. However, they are real and legitimate. You want to be in control of your own life.

If you have ever surfed the web, you have probably seen numerous scams suggesting that you can make thousands of dollars from home for doing practically nothing. Maybe you have gotten onto a website such as Craigslist looking for a way to work from home, only to find one scam after another. You are smart enough to know that you won't get paid for taking surveys or clicking on links. That's why you are looking at this eBook: you are looking for legitimate ways to work from home and earn income to support the lifestyle that you want.

The good news is that there are plenty of ways to earn income from home. This book will describe some of them to you and how you can get started. It will also detail some of the challenges associated with working from home, such as not having the socialization that is probably a part of your day job (even if you don't realize it), having to keep track of all of your income and expenses for tax purposes, and motivating yourself to stay on target.

Some of the topics covered include how to become a freelancer and what you should expect from different types of freelancing, starting your own online business, ways to generate passive income, and finding a home-based full-time job. It also contains a section on tips, and warnings to help you understand fully what you are getting into, when working from home and how to make the most of the challenges that you probably didn't anticipate.

If you are ready to understand how you can pursue the lifestyle that you want by working from home, then this is definitely the eBook for you. It provides a no-nonsense approach to the realities of working from home so that you are best prepared to get the most out of your new lifestyle. It will help you avoid scams and find legitimate work, in your own particular niche, that you will get paid for. Being able to work from home may sound too good to be true, but it isn't. Many people have successfully left their day jobs to pursue a career at home. You can join the ranks of those people, and this book will show you how.